I Can Read About®

Cats and Kittens

Written by Linda Murray • Illustrated by Fred Smith

Troll

People have kept cats and kittens as pets for centuries. Pictures of cats can be found in ancient Egyptian tombs, and farmers have always relied on cats to hunt mice and rats. But did you know that house cats are related to lions, tigers, and cheetahs?

Big powerful cats and small cuddly cats all belong to the *felidae* (FEE-lih-day), or cat, family. Lions and house cats share many of the same traits.

All cats are meat eaters. House cats hunt mice and other small animals. Big cats hunt large animals such as deer and wild sheep. They also hunt rabbits and birds if bigger prey is not available.

Cats have powerful jaws and thirty sharp teeth that bite and hold prey.

Most cats prefer to hunt at night. They have large eyes with fast-moving muscles that help them see well in dim light. Cats have sharp hearing that helps them find prey, and they also have a keen sense of smell.

All cats have five claws on each front paw and four on each back paw. The fifth claw on a cat's front paw is called a *dewclaw*.

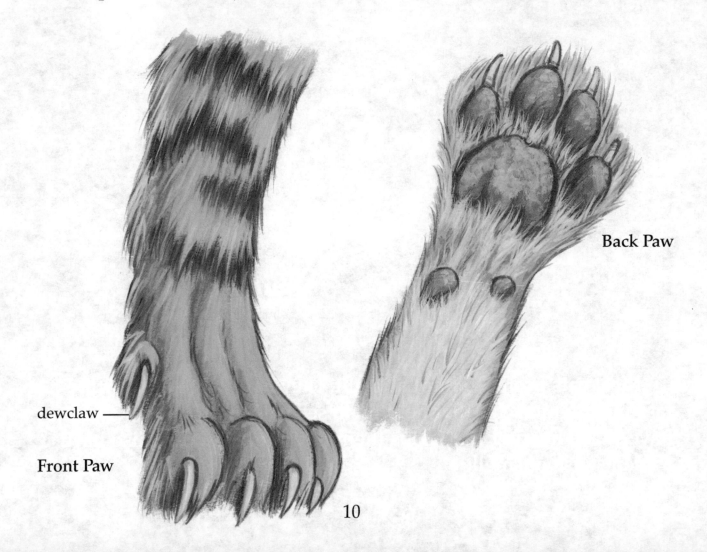

dewclaw —

Front Paw

Back Paw

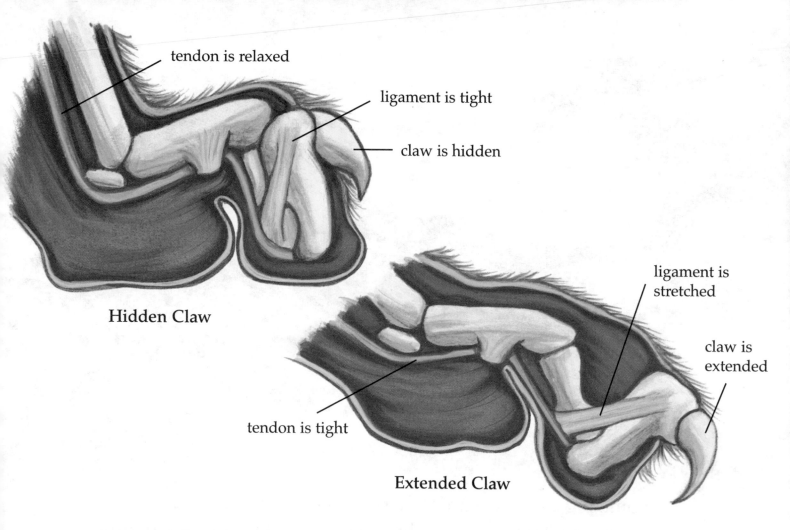

tendon is relaxed

ligament is tight

claw is hidden

Hidden Claw

ligament is stretched

claw is extended

tendon is tight

Extended Claw

Most of the time the claws are hidden. But when a cat spreads its toes, the sharp claws spring out.

Some big cats are extremely fast. The cheetah can run 60 miles (97 kilometers) per hour in a burst of speed. Lions can run only about 35 miles (56 kilometers) per hour, so they have to rely on their strength to catch prey.

House cats can run up to 30 miles (48 kilometers) per hour for short periods of time.

Some cats purr, while other cats roar. The house cat purrs. Wild cats such as the puma, lynx, bobcat, and ocelot also purr. All of these cats have a small bone at the base of their tongue that allows them to make this sound.

But many big cats, such as lions, tigers, leopards, jaguars, and cheetahs, do not have this bone, so they roar when they want to be heard!

15

Between hunting trips, cats sleep a lot. The mighty lion sometimes sleeps up to nineteen hours a day.

House cats can sleep up to sixteen hours a day, even though they simply have to walk to a feeding dish to eat. That's because the instinct to find a warm spot and curl up for a nap has been part of the cat's nature for centuries.

The first true members of the cat family lived about 40 million years ago—during the time of the dinosaurs! One of these cats, Smilodon, had long, razor-sharp fangs that hung from its jaw. Smilodon needed these big teeth to hunt huge prehistoric animals.

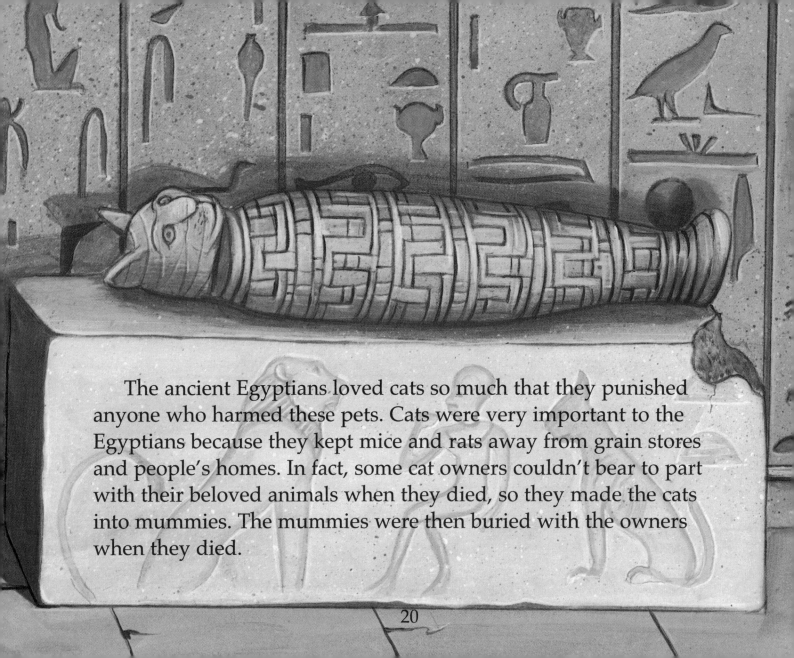

The ancient Egyptians loved cats so much that they punished anyone who harmed these pets. Cats were very important to the Egyptians because they kept mice and rats away from grain stores and people's homes. In fact, some cat owners couldn't bear to part with their beloved animals when they died, so they made the cats into mummies. The mummies were then buried with the owners when they died.

Today, people all over the world are fond of cats. For a long time, dogs were the most popular pets in the United States, but now the cat is the number-one pet. Many people find cats easier to take care of: they don't have to be walked, they require less attention than dogs, and they can be left for a day or two if their owner has to be away for a short period.

Some people think cats aren't as lovable as dogs, but cat owners will tell you these mysterious animals can be sweet and playful.

There are many different types of house, or *domestic*, cats.
Some popular purebred types include Siamese, Persian,
Russian Blue, and Manx.

Siamese cats have bright blue eyes and dark marks, or "points." These elegant-looking pets have a loud, mournful-sounding meow that tells their owners they want some attention!

The Persian, with its long, silky fur, is the most popular breed of cat. It is also one of the oldest breeds. People wrote about the Persian cat more than 3,600 years ago!

The Russian Blue's name comes from its unusual coat, which is short, thick, and a beautiful blue-gray color. In addition, the end of each hair looks as if it has been dipped in silver.

Most people can easily recognize the Manx cat because it doesn't have a tail!

There are also thousands of mixed-breed cats that are favorite
family pets. These cats have a wide variety of markings, and they come
in lots of colors, including black, brown, white, gray, and orange.
Many of these cats are just as beautiful as their purebred relatives.

If you were going to get a pet cat, which would you choose? It doesn't matter whether a cat is a purebred or a mixed breed. You can get an adult cat, or you might decide to get a kitten. Any cat will make a good pet if you take care of it and give it lots of love.

If you decide to get a kitten, make sure the kitten is the right age. Two to three months old is best. Look for a lively kitten that has clear eyes and a smooth coat.

Have your kitten examined by a veterinarian as soon as possible. It is important to make sure your kitten is vaccinated against certain feline diseases.

At first, feed your kitten two to three times a day. Young cats six months to one year old should be fed twice a day. Make sure your cat always has fresh water.

Show your kitten its bathroom—the litter box. Place the kitten in the box after it eats, and gently help the kitten scratch the litter with its paw so it gets used to how the litter feels. Change the litter once a week.

Kittens are playful and curious, and they love to be petted. It is also important to let your kitten be around other people so it will get used to humans. This interaction will help your kitten to be friendlier as it grows up.

A cat is easy to care for. It keeps itself clean by washing its fur with its rough tongue. Some long-haired cats will need to be bathed every few months to keep their coats in good condition. Cats that go outside may also need an occasional bath if their fur becomes very dirty.

Perhaps a cat you know will have kittens. The babies grow for nine weeks before they are born. The mother will find a warm, quiet place when it is time for her kittens to be born.

The mother licks the new kittens with her rough tongue to clean them and to start their breathing.

Their eyes are shut, their ears are just tiny flaps, and they cannot smell very well. They know where the mother is because they can feel her purring.

The kittens drink only their mother's milk for the first few weeks. During that time, their eyes and ears open, and they eat and grow.

When they are about four weeks old, the kittens will begin to eat solid food and to drink water. They are also ready for gentle play with their litter mates and with humans.

Kittens grow fast. When they are eight or nine weeks old, they are ready to go to new homes.

Someday you may welcome a kitten or cat into your home. Remember to take good care of it and give it lots of hugs and love, and you will have a faithful friend for life.

Index